Mother's Day 2008

Love, Mommy

A Mother's Journey Through Grief

JULIE S. DOMOGALLA

INKWATER PRESS

Cover & interior designed by Tricia Sgrignoli/Positive Images

Front cover photo © by Julie S. Domogalla
Belgian Lace II © istockphoto, Mary Lane
Bear & Blocks © bigstockphoto, Carolyne Pehora
Blocks © bigstockphoto, Garth Williams

www.inkwaterpress.com

ISBN 978-1-59299-190-7

Publisher: Inkwater Press

Printed in the U.S.A.

This is an account of my grief journey following the death of two of my children. Some people have asked what makes my experience different than others? Maybe that is the reason I feel compelled to write– because others may find a connection to their own grief. Still others have cautioned me, fearing that the project and my journey back into the grief will take me to the dark places in my heart where the scars have formed. They fail to understand I am in those places regularly. It is a part of me.

Yet something urged me on to share my story– my journey from the depths of dismal grief to the rediscovery of joy in my life– to a place where my heart can once again truly sing. I pray those of you struggling with loss, may find comfort and hope. No one can truly appreciate your journey. I only hope that my words may comfort you in your grieving, in your own way, at your own time.

God Bless you.

JULIE S. DOMOGALLA

Acknowledgments

This book was written to honor the memory of my children, Kevin and Jill. It also honors the memory of my Uncle Leon Westendorf who was the first to encourage me to share my journal and story with others.

There are so many people to thank for their support, encouragement and expertise. Thank you to my editors, Sonia Albers and Tammy Olson. Thank you to Dr Stephen Kurachek who was with me in those dark days and continued to support my vision for this project many years later. Thank you to my family and friends for their love and support. Thank you to my dear husband, Scott, who has always encouraged me to follow my dreams. Finally, I thank God for grace abundant.

Table of Contents

Chapter 1
Clouded Joy

Shortly after 2 A.M., I woke with a start. I knew that familiar pressure building in my abdomen. I raced to the bathroom where my water broke. Since this was my second pregnancy and I was three days overdue, I wasn't alarmed. I went back to bed to lie down. No need to act until the contractions were more regular. As I laid there in the dark, wondering about this little life that was soon to join our family, I could not possibly know how this day, July 7, 1986, would so drastically change my life.

Daybreak came and the contractions were still not close enough to warrant a trip to the hospital. At 10 A.M. I decided to call the doctor's office. The nurse spoke with great urgency, telling me to come to the hospital at once. So I gathered my things and found a baby-sitter for my oldest son, who was just one month shy of his second birthday. My husband and I drove to the hospital and waited.

Finally, the time came for our child to be born. It was mid afternoon. I recall the labor as being unremarkable. What I do remember very clearly is the doctor's words upon the birth of our second son. "We have some trouble with the lower appendages," followed by the shock when he said, "Oh my God, he has no arms either!"

Kevin, as we named him, cried immediately as the doctor held his little body. The nurses flew into the room in numbers. Suddenly, our quiet delivery turned into pandemonium. My husband collapsed onto my still swollen stomach, sobbing and saying, "Oh my God, look at him, just look at him!" These were the same words he had uttered when our first son was born, but the meaning was entirely different.

I tried to see what was happening. I was in total shock and, quite frankly, at a distinct disadvantage to see what the commotion was. I remember having a quick glance of Kevin before he was whisked away. Kevin was born with no arms. His legs were a total of two inches long, each consisting of a fleshy, fingerlike appendage ending in one curled toe. They looked like little elf shoes– his whole leg looked like a little elf shoe.

My husband continued to sob on my stomach as I delivered the afterbirth. I just kept saying, "We will get through this– it will be all right." I wasn't confident about my words or feelings, but I would not allow myself to lose control. Kevin needed me. I struggled to keep myself composed. I was afraid if I fell apart, we would lose control of the situation. No one was calm in that room, with the exception of the doctor and myself.

In the midst of that chaos, I tried to stay calm and remember the moment when I had called Kevin's name. He had turned and looked at me. He looked straight into my eyes, knowing my voice. It was just for a precious second before he was taken from my room, but it was the one precious moment I held on to in the days ahead.

This birth took place in a small-town hospital in the community of Bloomer, WI. Clearly, they had never had a case such as this, so I wasn't surprised when they transferred Kevin to a newborn ICU in nearby Eau Claire. They would not allow me to go with him. Everyone left and I was alone in that hospital room. The nurse came in to check on me about an hour later. She asked if there was anything she could get me. I could see the tears in her eyes. I asked her for paper and a pen or pencil. That was the moment I knew that I had to write about this experience. It wasn't a long thought-out decision. God laid it out plainly for me to see.

Dear Kevin,

Mommy is so sad right now. I want to hold you and kiss you and let you know how much you are loved. I haven't even touched you, except for a brief brush of your face. I am scared about what will happen now. I know it won't be easy, but I love you very much and will do my best. Your big brother loves you even if he does not understand.

There are many kinds of pain in this life. You will find that out my son. Yet, there are many joyful, wonderful things as well. I am hoping we can share those together.

This is a moment when we need to ask God for his help and direction. I know He hears us and loves us. It is so hard to have faith when things don't go as we planned. That's when we need Him even more.

So, my precious little one, I grieve for not being with you now, but know in my heart we will be together soon.

I love you.

Love,

Mommy

I listened to the other babies crying down the hall. People called and offered to come and sit with me, but I told them I was okay. That was how the pattern of my grief was going to be– me telling everyone I was okay, while I was really dying inside.

I slept little and prayed often through the night. The next morning a dear, silver-haired woman peered into my door. She was a member of the hospital auxiliary. She had tears in her eyes just like the nurse the night before. She told me they had gifts for all the newborns, but she hesitated to show me. It was a pair of hand knit booties. "I suppose you do not have any use for these," she hesitated. We both cried and I thanked her.

I got dressed and waited for the doctor to see me. He did see me for a brief visit and I was released; walking out by 9 A.M. I was going to be with my son!

All through my pregnancy I had told everyone that this baby was not as active as my first child. The doctor was not concerned, but suggested I lie down twice a day and count movement. The baby did move, but more in a twisting sort of way rather than any sharp kicks. I explained that to the doctor. Neither of us dreamed of the reason I felt these strange movements.

During those next few days, as word spread of Kevin's birth, many people questioned how we did not know he would be born this way. I was repeatedly asked why I didn't notice a difference. My response was always the same– that I did notice a difference, talked with my doctor about it, and dismissed it as not a real concern. We had no health insurance at the time. My husband was enrolled in a Lutheran Seminary; then serving as an intern pastor in this small town; so I did not elect to do the routine ultrasound.

Finances were tight. We had considered an ultrasound at 7-1/2 months because Kevin was in a breech position. He turned four days before the ultrasound appointment, so it was canceled. I thank God for that gift. It was a shock when he was born, but the agony of those last weeks knowing my unborn child was significantly physically challenged were spared.

After the first twenty or so people questioned how I could not know my baby would have no arms or legs, I got a little defensive. It started feeling accusatory. I now understand that people want answers to questions to calm their fears of uncertainty. It reassures them (albeit falsely) that this could never happen to them. At the time, it was very difficult to accept.

In addition, there was the barrage of questions from doctors and concerned others about what I had done to make this happen. Family history? Drugs or medications taken while pregnant? Pesticides? Harmful exposures to radiation? Similarities and parallels were drawn to thalidomide children born in the 1950s with their absence of limbs or severely deformed limbs. One doctor even commented to me how surprised he was that I had not miscarried Kevin early in my pregnancy. Not only was I a failure as a mother because I bore a physically challenged son, but I was also a failure because I should have not carried him to full term. I didn't need to hear that. I heard more about thalidomide babies than I cared to. I just wanted to care for my newborn son. The reason why he was that way wasn't particularly important to me. It seemed to be a lot of other peoples' focus and I could not appreciate why.

Kevin stayed only two days in that ICU. He was able to nurse and only needed low levels of oxygen. I recall the doctor asking us if we were certain we wanted to keep Kevin. There were other options. I had never considered I would not take this child home with me. I was driven to start caring for him myself. That's what mothers do.

Dear Kevin,

I remember that drive to the hospital to bring you home. We weren't even sure how to put you in the car seat. It seemed there were so many things to learn! The doctor asked us if we wanted one more day to get used to the idea that you had no limbs.

He also asked us if we were sure we wanted to keep you. I could not imagine not wanting you. You see, Mommy never saw you as a freak. You were my little Kevin.

We had your picture taken in the hospital and we took you home. Mommy was so nervous and elated at the same time. We were flooded with neighbors and friends who stopped by.

You are so adorable. Your eyes are dark blue and seem to reflect so much compassion. You have that full head of curly dark brown hair. I love to comb it with my fingers as I rock you. It wraps around my little finger. I talked to you today and you turned to my voice...at the age of two whole days. I love you so much.

Love,

Mommy

After we brought Kevin home, we tried to resume a *normal* family life. The four of us– my husband and I, our nearly two-year-old son, and this newborn baby who faced so many challenges– living together and trying to make sense of it all. I was fortunate in those first four weeks of Kevin's life. All the doctors and nurses had assured me that short of Kevin's obvious handicaps, he was a very healthy baby.

Taking care of Kevin was a challenge in some ways. I remember struggling at times when giving him a bath. He had no arms or legs to hold onto and he would wiggle away from me. It was difficult to hold onto him. I tried to be so careful. Kevin cried; almost screamed, when I bathed his small feet-like appendages. I trimmed his one toenail and that really seemed to bother him. I am not sure if they were extra sensitive or why he disliked that. Since he did not like anyone touching him on his legs, we struggled with how to place him in a car seat with the straps that go between the legs. We improvised, using a lot of extra blankets rolled up on either side of him. It was just a guess.

There was no need for two-piece outfits for Kevin. He weighed five pounds eleven ounces at birth. His torso was the size of a full-term eight-pound baby, but he weighed less due to no appendages. He had a narrow chest cavity and body so he wore preemie sized diapers. I soon found out that newborn onezie outfits were the perfect match. With his little body fitted in a short-sleeved, one-piece outfit, he was comfortable and could move when he wanted. Sleepers had to be pinned up or tied in some crazy configuration, so I quickly stopped using them.

Dear Kevin,

You are over a week old and doing great! I am so excited about all your dark curly hair. You did not sleep well last night so we will both be tired today. Your brother Jimmy is so helpful. He sure thinks you are special. So do I!

Love,
Mommy

In the nights following his birth, I had a recurring dream of delivering a baby. The baby was born without any limbs. I would wake up in horror only to realize it was not a dream, but my ever-present reality. Then I would remember the feeling of giving birth. Kevin came out with one push. Once his head was free, the rest of him came quickly. His shoulders were very small as there were no arms attached, and his chest cavity was underdeveloped. I live with a vivid memory of the absence of feeling those shoulders and legs come out of my body. When you deliver a baby, the doctor usually pauses after the head and works out one shoulder at a time. I had felt my other child's legs come out. I can recall the feeling of Kevin's delivery at this writing, many years later. I will never forget how that felt. Even now, the horror of it is still with me.

There was much work to do finding assistance from such resources such as Social Security benefits and Shriners Hospital. The paperwork seemed to overwhelm me, but I kept persisting. We met with officials at the Social Security office when Kevin was just two weeks old. They could not determine if he was disabled. We had him with us and it was pretty obvious to me he had some disabilities! They would not call for four more weeks to tell us he had been determined to be labeled: *disabled.* He would be dead by then. The notification of his acceptance by the Shriners would also come after his death, but at least this process was handled with compassion. I have always been grateful for that.

Kevin and I had some wonderful days. Kevin responded to me at such an early age. He smiled at less than a week old. He rolled over– front to back and back to front– at the age of two weeks. He would lift his little bottom off the floor and twist himself over. He could do the same with his head. I would watch him, simply amazed, and marvel. These were the same movements he must have been making in my womb. He had been perfecting this twisting motion for months and now that he was out in the world with no arms or legs to get in his way, he was using it to his advantage. If I walked by him and said something, he turned his head to follow me. If that did not satisfy him, he would turn over to change his vantage point.

I had been writing to Kevin all along. It started with a single piece of paper handed to me by the nurse in the hospital where he was born. I was soon writing to him on every scrap of paper I could find. I bought myself one of those blank books for writing. I had always planned on rewriting all my loose papers in the book. That never happened, as each of those loose papers is too precious for me to part with.

My favorite picture of Kevin (and I have plenty!) is one I took of him and his older brother Jim just after a bath. I had just put him down on the carpet when Jim laid down next to him to talk to him. I ran to get the camera, hoping for a shot of the two of them looking at one another. But when I said Jim's name, Kevin turned toward me, giving me a wonderful picture of the two of them with Kevin's eyes wide open and alert. All this from a baby three weeks old.

Dear Kevin,

I have a favorite photograph of you. It is the one of you and your brother lying on the floor together. I keep it with me wherever I go. Your uncle tells me he keeps a copy with him too. He says when things get rough and he gets down, he turns to that picture and it helps him feel better. You are an inspiration to so many people.

Love,

Mommy

We continued life with Kevin, planning for his baptism, which we had scheduled before his birth. He was just shy of one month old. By now the news of his birth had reached people well beyond our small community. Relatives in all corners of the country had shared his birth with others and showers of prayers came our way. We prayed for a miracle– not that he would suddenly sprout arms and legs, but that he would have a life that was full. I prayed for the strength and faith to continue on as a mother. I was not naive. I knew I had some very difficult days to face. Many professionals had already told me that Kevin would never walk and would be confined to a wheelchair for his life. They also told me he would not have a normal life, but could still have some quality of life. What exactly did that mean? I would ask and the answers were always to wait and see what developed.

I found myself in those few short weeks being flooded with cards and well wishes. I cherished the time alone with my two boys. Since there was no one I could call to answer the questions of bathing and car seats, I went on instinct.

We were fortunate to have many people who cared for us as a family. I was given a special gift of hours with my two boys, Kevin and Jim. And in the still of the night, it was just Kevin and I sharing the quiet. Kevin would not cry long. I now understand why that was, but I didn't at the time. He was struggling to breathe.

Friends of ours had a baby boy just a few days after Kevin was born. He was perfect. I would be lying if I said that did not hurt. It hurt me deeply.

Dear Kevin,

I saw our friend's new baby. It hurt so much to look at him. He looked so perfect and when he wiggled his little toes, I died inside. Oh my wee little one, I hurt so badly.

Sometimes I think I am doing so well. I am trying so hard to be strong and accepting; it just isn't easy.

Love,

Mommy

Insensitive remarks left their scars on my heart as well. The most blatant came when an elderly neighbor lady came to call. We had moved into our house a year before Kevin's birth. She lived close by yet I had never met her. One afternoon, she came to my door and knocked. When I opened the door, she simply said, "Hello. I am your neighbor and I heard you had a baby." I replied that, yes, I had a new baby. She stood on the step not saying anything, creating an awkward moment. I finally asked if she would like to come in, which she did. She looked around and asked, "Where is he?" Kevin was sleeping in a stroller as we had just returned from a walk. I pointed to the stroller explaining that he was asleep. He was bundled up in a blanket like most small babies. She asked to see him. I told her he was right there. Then she asked if she could see him. I told her he was sleeping, I was busy making supper, and that she would have to excuse me. She sat for a while and finally left. There were no words of congratulation or sympathy. No gift or card. Only someone who wanted to get a look at my son, the one she considered a freak. It was a very difficult day for me.

But then there were good days, like the day I went shopping for something to wear at Kevin's baptism. I had him all wrapped in a blanket in the stroller as I went on that impossible task of shopping for a dress– only three weeks after having a baby. Ugh! I recall the store clerk who was helping me commented on how beautiful and perfect he was. She had no idea Kevin had challenges. I didn't tell her any different. It was almost a dreamlike moment– not too different from the dream of finding a dress that would fit my body that day!

The day of Kevin's baptism was beautiful. I had asked a couple who were friends of ours if they would honor us by being sponsors. Of course, she and I both cried. My family came for the service and a potluck dinner was held in honor of Kevin that day. We had so many people encouraging us. We were filled with hope that day.

I took Kevin to a scheduled one-month checkup at my doctor's office just a few days later. Despite all the differences Kevin had physically, there were no medical appointments between his two-day stay in ICU and this regular one-month checkup. I thought little of it at the time, but now I truly believe there was fear or apprehension on the part of his caregivers. They just were not sure what to do with him.

As our family doctor and I talked, he started sounding a little defensive as I questioned how neither of us knew about Kevin's limbs before birth. I had to reassure him that lawsuits were not part of my plan and that he could share openly with me. What an awkward situation that was.

The doctor noticed that Kevin's color was not as pink as it should be. They had said the same at the ICU unit when he was born, but had said that he would *pink right up* on oxygen. I often wondered why they didn't send Kevin home with oxygen.

During the course of this one-month checkup, the doctor detected a heart murmur. He ordered an X-ray, but could see nothing right away. He then ordered a consultation with a pediatric cardiac specialist at the Minneapolis Heart Institute– a two-hour drive away. We set the appointment for two days later, as he felt there was no immediate urgency.

I walked out of the doctor's office and got into the car. I held Kevin in my arms, closed the door and screamed. I cried and screamed for some time. It was a hot day and the car was stuffy inside. But I kept the windows rolled tight as my very soul screamed in pain; the tears and sweat rolling down my face. Kevin just lay quietly in my arms while his mother slowly went out of her mind with grief and fear.

The next day was my oldest son Jim's second birthday. I tried to make it as normal of a day as I could. We played a happy birthday record on the stereo over and over. Jim was dancing the whole time. I baked a cake and shaped it into a truck. I tried to dye the frosting into a red color so it would look like a fire engine, but he ended up with a pink truck. He loved it anyway. Kevin was fussy that day, but he seldom cried for long. Still, I did not appreciate why.

I got up the next morning, full of fear. It was the day of the appointment with the cardiac specialist. My husband and I drove to my parents' home where we left Jim to play. Kevin was sick to his stomach in the car. I figured it was just the car ride. By the time we made it to the appointment we were all very nervous. The doctor immediately noted Kevin's color saying he was cyanotic. When I interrupted him to ask him what exactly he meant, he yelled at me. He claimed the tension in the room was unbearable. Yes, there was a great deal of tension in that room. We were terrified that our son's life was in jeopardy.

Kevin vomited again while the doctor examined him. The doctor ordered an X-ray of his chest and, later, an echocardiogram. I stayed with Kevin the entire time. My husband waited outside, reading the newspaper. That was a pattern that developed and repeated. He would watch TV or read somewhere, removed from the immediate scene while I would stay as long as I could by Kevin's side.

The tests were inconclusive, yet the doctor still gave a diagnosis of Persistent Fetal Circulation– an immature heart condition where a hole remains open after birth. It often corrects itself– if not, surgery is required to close the hole in the heart. The doctor assured us it was a fairly common condition. The doctor scheduled an appointment for one month later to examine whether or not the condition had improved on its own. He told us to watch for a change in Kevin's color (which he had already told us was not good), poor eating habits (I told him Kevin had slowed down on his eating and would not nurse on my right side), and labored breathing. We left with the doctor's assurance that this was not a crisis situation– there was no need for immediate concern. Now I truly was confused. I was still concerned and had not found the reassurance I had hoped for.

Chapter 2

Saying Good-bye

We drove back to my parent's home and decided to stay the night, as we were all exhausted. That was one of the worst nights for Kevin. I was up most of the night trying to soothe him. He wouldn't eat and would cry until his color was gray. Then he would rest for twenty minutes or so before it would begin again. I was scared I might lose him that night, even though the specialist had just told me there was no immediate danger.

We returned home the next morning and I did my best to care for Kevin. He still wasn't eating. Breathing was even more difficult for him. I called the emergency room at our local small-town hospital where he was born and talked with the doctor who was on call for emergencies. When I told him that Kevin had not kept anything down for over twenty-four hours, he suggested we bring him in. After examining Kevin, he called the same specialist in Minneapolis who had seen Kevin the day before. They argued over the phone until the emergency room doctor convinced him that Kevin needed immediate care. They set up a bed for him at the Life Support Unit (ICU) at Minneapolis Children's Hospital. The next few days would be some of the most difficult days of my life.

A friend drove Kevin and me to the Children's Hospital in Minneapolis– some 120 miles away. I talked with Kevin most of the way. We arrived at the hospital and told the receptionist at the front desk that we were expected in the ICU unit. There was some confusion as I was not familiar with the term of Life Support Unit. She called the Neonatal ICU, but they were not expecting Kevin. We stood in the lobby for ten minutes waiting to find out where to go. Kevin looked grayer by the minute. Finally, the receptionist sent us to the LSU unit right across the lobby.

The unit was a large open area. There were many beds in separate areas divided by curtains. In the center was a nurse's station. The nurses put Kevin in a small bed in the front of the unit on the far side of the entry. They asked me to wait outside while the doctor examined him and put in an IV. Reluctantly, I waited outside. I sent my friend back home, telling her I was okay. It was a pattern I would take in the days ahead. Then I was alone– and terrified.

Dear Kevin,

It is funny how I was looking in my purse just now and ran across the letter I wrote to you the day you were born. It has been over a month and things are still very tough. I am at Children's Hospital because you haven't been keeping anything down. We were just here yesterday for a heart exam and now we are back in the city again.

I am so scared, my little one, and so exhausted. I did not sleep last night and I am not sure I will tonight either. When you look into my eyes, I know how confused you must be. What a bombardment at such a young age. You, my little man, have suffered more than I in my lifetime of twenty-four years. I ache so for you.

I have cried so much I almost feel numb– I just cannot feel anymore because it hurts too much. Oh dear God, could I please have a miracle?

Love,

Mommy

When the nurse led me back into the unit to see Kevin, I was not at all prepared for what I saw. He was on oxygen, which I expected. But when I saw the IV coming out of the top of his tiny little head, I was devastated. He had no hands or feet to connect the IV to. They had shaved off most of his curly top hair and there were several places where you could see the unsuccessful IV attempts. His forehead and head were swollen and red. There were monitors attached to his tiny little body. There was so little of him that was not somehow covered with an attached tube or wire. Now he did look like some creature from another world, like others had hinted. I knew then I was losing control of my son's care. Somehow, he looked even smaller and frailer than he did when I had carried him in. My heart sank as I sat down at his bedside.

Dear Kevin,

How Mommy aches for you! They put the IV on the right side of your head. That is the only side you can sleep on. I tried to tell them so, but they said they had tried the left side. They also tried putting it in your neck and it is all swollen and red. You poor little thing. You look so beat up by the world. I just ache to hold you, but these things are all attached to you and Mommy cannot move you without the nurse's help. I am so scared.

Why is God doing this to us?

Love,

Mommy

It was during these dark minutes I was introduced to the specialist who would change the course of my experience at the hospital. His name was Dr. Kurachek. He was a pediatric pulmonologist and director of the unit. He spoke softly and carefully to me. He told me he was concerned Kevin was dehydrated and in chronic need of oxygen. He explained his condition could be the result of a virus. I asked if I could hold Kevin; he agreed, and the nurses helped me. As I was holding him, the oxygen tube kept coming out of his nose. I was so afraid he would die in my arms, because of my selfish need to hold him. I asked them to lay him back down with the oxygen tent over him instead. I had completely lost the option to care for my son. It was out of my hands.

Somehow I was not convinced Dr. Kurachek was telling me the whole story. My sister arrived about 12:30 A.M. that night. She had been at a neighboring hospital where she worked as a registered nurse. The doctor talked to her much differently than me. Maybe he held back some possibilities because I was alone. It helped so much to have my sister there. We talked about the gadgets attached to Kevin. She explained some of the reasons why they kept taking chest X-rays and blood gas tests. Dr. Kurachek and my sister convinced me I should rest for a while. Kevin was stable and needed his rest. He was too weak to nurse, so once again I was not needed. Mothers are supposed to be needed by their little ones.

Dear Kevin,

Mommy keeps thinking of the way you looked at me in the hospital tonight. I was so terrified; yet you seemed so calm.

I know you heard me and listened to me. Was that trust in your eyes?

Love,
Mommy

I left the hospital about 1:30 A.M. with my sister. She lived only a few blocks from the hospital, so I stayed with her. I remember lying awake wondering what was happening to my little boy. The doctor had promised to call if anything changed. I wanted to be there so badly, but everyone told me I should get some rest. I listened to them.

I woke early the next morning and was back at the hospital by 6 A.M. Kevin had slept and the news was encouraging. The nurse was going to try to feed him some liquid nourishment. I asked if I could do it instead and she was agreed. I had no idea that would be the last time I would hold my son before he died in my arms.

Dear Kevin,

I remember how you looked at me after you drank all that water. You almost smiled and gazed at me with such a look of contentment. That is the last moment I have of you truly alive. I held you for so long that morning. I did not want to let go.

Love,
Mommy

It was a Sunday morning when friends and relatives showed up at the hospital in force! My parents, my husband and our older son Jim, and my sister-in-law crowded around this tiny bed in the intensive care unit. The nurse finally asked some to leave as we had quite a group in that room. It was wonderful to have their support; I was starting to feel reassured. Then, Dr. Kurachek took my husband and me aside. He explained that the tests were showing that Kevin had a serious condition called Pulmonary Hypertension. There is no cure short of a heart and lung transplant. They do not perform such transplants on infants. The best we could hope for would be to try to give Kevin some quality of life for the remainder of what time he had. I wanted to die right there on that chair.

I went outside for a walk with my sister and my son Jim. The others left the hospital. There was nothing anyone could do now– except pray. I wasn't even certain I could do that. My husband went back to my sister's apartment for a nap. I could not imagine how he could sleep. A couple of hours later, I went to get him and we walked back into the unit. What we saw as we walked in will remain forever a vivid nightmare.

Surrounding this tiny month-old infant was a team of doctors and nurses. They were using an ambu bag to breathe for him. My husband and I were escorted out of the unit and asked to wait outside. The waiting seemed like forever. Dr. Kurachek finally found us waiting outside and explained that they had to put a ventilator on Kevin because he was not breathing on his own. He further explained that Kevin was sedated and would not feel any pain. He told us it might be time to consider whether this was quality of life and that we may need to make decisions about disconnecting the ventilator. I immediately told him to take it off. I knew in my heart that Kevin belonged in heaven– not on some breathing machine in a hospital. But there were hoops to jump through before we could make such a determination. The doctor explained the issue would need to be brought to an ethics committee in two days where a team of doctors, therapists, and ministers would examine whether or not it was morally sound to disconnect Kevin's life support. I was outraged! Not only was I not able to care for my son as a mother should, but my ability to speak for him as a patient was gone as well.

Dear Kevin,

I remember walking into that unit to see you after meeting with the doctor. It was a horrible sight. Your head now had a swollen bruise on it where they had attempted the IV on the left side. You were motionless except for the ventilator breathing air in and out of your tiny body. It made your stomach swell. You were gone to me. At that moment you were already gone.

Love,

Mommy

I stayed right by Kevin's side, tired of everyone telling me I needed to leave or get rest. My husband went out to the lobby. He sat out there watching television or reading. Sometimes, there were others to talk to. But I would not leave Kevin. He was not going to be alone because these might be the last few hours we would have together. I needed that.

At 10:30 P.M., I left for a few minutes to use the bathroom. When I walked back into the unit, they were once again using an ambu bag to keep Kevin breathing. The doctor told me there was no need for the ethics committee to convene. Kevin would probably not make it through the next hour. Even the respirator was not enough to keep him alive.

I stayed by his side until 3A.M. Kevin and I were alone in that large open unit. My whole world was confined to a small area that was surrounded by colorless curtains. My breasts were swollen from not nursing my son for over two days. I had no breast pump and had to ask for a set of scrubs to wear. My breasts had leaked through my clothes and I had nothing else to wear. The nurse and my husband convinced me to lie down for a short time. I was exhausted, but feared for the worse. Every time I left it seemed that Kevin got worse. While it did not occur to me at the time, I have since wondered if he was waiting for me to give him permission to die. I was trying so desperately to hang on to the few moments I had left. Kevin was ready to go– maybe I was just not ready to have him leave me.

When I came back into the unit after resting for two hours, they told me Kevin had improved. Now what was I supposed to feel? Improved to what, I thought. He was still restricted to these machines with no chance of any life beyond that. He was sedated and totally unaware of his surroundings. What did *improvement* mean?

Dear Kevin,

There are only hours left now. I never imagined I could hurt as much as I do. I am still so scared for everyone who loves you.

I am so scared for you too. I know there is something better waiting for you. God will take care of you. I just wanted to take care of you for a little longer.

I love you so much. I wish I could know that you understand that now.

Good-bye.

Love,
Mommy

That morning dragged on as I sat by his side. They were constantly taking blood samples to test for the gas ratio in Kevin's blood. When the doctor on call read the test that morning, he was encouraged by the results and directed the nurse to change the rate of oxygen from 100% to 75% oxygen and 25% CO2.

That was the turning point. It was 11:30A.M. on Monday, August 11, 1987. Kevin's heart rate dropped drastically and the nurse quickly turned up the oxygen content, but it was too late. Alarms started going off and I quickly sent my sister out to get my husband. They asked me to step back as they started using an ambu bag on Kevin's small frail body. One of the nurses suggested I leave. I refused. I was not leaving again!

We stood and watched this team of professionals as they tried to save the tiny body that was lying on the bed. My husband cried and I started speaking out. "You bastards," I said, "Can't you see he is meant to die? Why are you trying to play God? Please let him go!"

The doctor on duty calmly walked away from Kevin and called Dr. Kurachek. He explained that he had a mother *near hysteria.* He further explained Kevin's condition. If they needed to see hysteria to let my son go, then that's what they would get!

After a short phone consultation, the doctors agreed to stop all medications with the exception of the sedative. Dr. Kurachek arrived a few minutes later and after examining Kevin, agreed to allow Kevin to die. We assembled around Kevin's bedside: I, my husband, our son Jim, my sister, and a friend and pastor, Bob Albers, from St. Paul. The pastor said a prayer and the nurse began removing monitor patches and IVs. I asked if I could help, and she shook her head quietly in agreement. I was freeing my son from the artificial world that would not allow him to go home to heaven. This was definitely something I could do for my son! Finally, it was time to become his mother again. The nurse loosened the tape around Kevin's mouth where the ventilator tube was and I gently pulled it out, giving him his freedom to go to our Father in Heaven. I cannot begin to describe what a powerful moment that was for me. I gave him the very best gift I could– the permission to die.

I wrapped him in a blanket and sat in the rocking chair at the side of his bed. I held him for a long time. My husband held him and my son kissed him, but I asked for him back right away. I just rocked him and cried and said good-bye. Everyone else left. I wanted to be alone with my son, just like the nights we had spent alone during that short month of his life. I stayed there a long time. By now my tiny little son was a battered lifeless body. There was a large swollen bruise on one side of his head and the little hair he had left after shaving could not cover it up. The color was all gone from his face and he lay there still and cold. I had no idea I could hurt so much, not just emotionally, but also that sharp physical pain. It was difficult to even draw a breath.

The nurse coaxed me to leave. It took her several attempts before I reluctantly gathered his few belongings and walked out of that ward. I knew it would be the last time I would hold my son. I thought the nightmare had ended and the healing could somehow begin. Little did I understand the direction this grief would take my life.

I don't recall the drive home. It seems that my life moved on for the next few days in a blur. I was aware of my surroundings and practical about what needed to be done. I have always turned to work or the task at hand in stressful situations. My grief was no different. Upon arriving home we had many concerned people from our church and our community. My husband and I met with the funeral home director and made some plans– certainly not the type of arrangements we ever planned to make for our child. He explained that infants of Kevin's size were not even required to have a vault. How could I pick out a casket for my precious little curly-headed boy? It was too much to ask of us, but we did it. Somehow we summoned the strength, courage, or just plain determination to do it.

We met with the pastor of our church Rev Huget, a wonderful caring man who tried to help us plan a funeral. He first suggested the hymn, "Children of the Heavenly Father". I immediately snapped back at him saying no, that I could not bear to hear my only surviving child sing that same song in Sunday school after it was sung at Kevin's funeral. He asked about scripture and I remembered that so many people, some I have never met to this day, sent cards of congratulations and condolences upon Kevin's birth. One professor at the Lutheran Seminary, where my husband was a student, sent the words, " I am so sorry to learn that your joy has been clouded."That was powerful to me then and it still is. I searched through the cards looking for the scripture references. (I had never included something like that on a card I sent to anyone. Realizing the comfort it brought me, I often now include them.)

I came upon the reference to Romans 8: "Nothing will be able to separate us from the love of God in Christ Jesus..."(Romans 8:38-39). It was fitting. We also picked the words from Luke where Jesus welcomed the children– even infants– despite the disciples' attempts to discourage it. "Let the children come to me, and do not hinder them; for to such belongs the kingdom of God" (Luke 18:16b).

Our pastor left and I searched through the hymnal for some idea of songs. I looked through the words to that old familiar hymn, "Children of the Heavenly Father" and even though I had initially objected, I decided there was nothing more appropriate. As I thumbed through the pages I came across an old hymn my mother first taught me. I used to play it on the piano when I was about twelve. "Blest Be the Tie That Binds". It speaks of Christian love and unity, of hope and joy, of compassion and shared sorrow. It was perfect. We asked our pastor's teenage son to sing it for us at the funeral.

I searched through Kevin's clothes to find something for him to wear. I am not sure why that was such an important decision for me to make, but it was. After a futile search, I sat down with my husband and we agreed that Kevin's happiest day was his baptism when we put all our faith and hope for the future in our Lord. I called my mother to ask how she felt about our idea. She made this baptismal gown when our oldest son was born, and intended it to be a family legacy. She cried. We all did a lot of that. She assured me it was okay– that it had been a joyous day, and it certainly was fitting that he be buried in it.

That taken care of, there was the question of where to bury Kevin. My mother-in-law had a plot in a cemetery in southern Wisconsin. My parents planned on being buried in their local cemetery, but had no plot. We lived in that small town in west central Wisconsin and knew we would only be there for a few more short weeks as my husband's internship was coming to an end and he would need to return to the Minneapolis-St. Paul area for his last year of seminary.

I felt so torn between which set of grandparents would have Kevin next to them. I had no idea where I would be buried someday. After all, you do not make those life decisions when you are twenty-four. As I was lamenting over this decision, a friend stopped in the house. His wife had died quite unexpectedly that winter. He said that there was room next to her in the local cemetery should we wish to use it. A prayer was answered. Kevin lived his short life in this little community and they loved him so dearly. It became an easy decision to make.

The funeral remains a blur to me. It was a large funeral. I remember looking at my little boy with makeup caked on the large bruise so it was not so obvious. I asked the funeral director to cut a lock of his hair for me and gave him an envelope and scissors. I am not sure where that idea came from, but I am so grateful for every tiny fragment of Kevin I have to hold on to. Pictures, journal entries, a lock of hair, some of his clothes, and even ink prints of the single toe from each of his legs.

Many people attended Kevin's funeral and offered their support– some were helpful, some were not. The pastor's message centered on Baptism and the gift of the Holy Spirit that Kevin had received just two weeks earlier. I recall his message clearly as he had the foresight to audio tape it for us. There was a woman who had also lost a daughter and told me that this was God's gift to me. Now I would be truly able to minister to those who lose a child. I certainly was not looking for that gift and I quickly excused myself from her. While she may have meant well, these certainly were not the words you give to someone in the utter despair of acute grief– at her son's funeral!

We buried Kevin with a cross necklace my husband had worn around his neck and a small teddy bear.

Dear Kevin,

We buried you today. It was such a long, awful day. Your big brother is so confused, and I have no idea how to explain all this to him. We buried you in your baptismal gown. I think it was the right decision, although I wonder if Jim will resent it when he has children. It was his first and meant to be passed on. When the funeral home director went to close your casket, he took your little teddy bear and cross and placed them at the bottom of the casket where your feet should be. I said, "No" and asked him to move them up by your face. I guess it seems silly to give you a teddy bear. I was so afraid you would get lonely and cold in that dark earth...and Mommy would not be there to hold you. But how will you hold the bear? You with no arms or hands to grasp? I just pray that you will be whole in heaven.

I am so sorry I did not realize how fragile you were. I should have known. I am your mother. I am so sorry I did not realize how fragile I am.

I am only beginning to discover that. It is horrible here without you.

Love,

Mommy

Chapter 3

Functioning Through the Grief

The days following the funeral were a blur as well. How I wandered through the minutes of those days is unclear. My family and I had a whirlwind of activity as we had to move west to the city of St. Paul just two weeks later. My husband had one more year of seminary to complete there. Here was another loss– the people who had been so supportive and caring during our struggle to save Kevin were now going to be over 100 miles away. But move we did, and three weeks after Kevin's death, I was back to working full time to support the family, while my husband struggled to finish his last year of seminary.

Those were some very dark days. I spent every possible minute I could with my remaining son, Jim. My husband sank into a deep depression. We isolated ourselves from one another. We could not seem to share in the grief. I would lay my son down for a nap in the early afternoon and leave for work. I would have horrific flashes in my mind that he would never wake again. I would have to call from work to make certain he was okay. After the long hours of work, I would race home to check on him once again.

I struggled with my weight. I certainly did not want to look like I had a baby, yet I found some type of strange comfort in holding on to the weight. It reminded me of happier days before Kevin was born. I was twenty-four years old and my hair started turning gray. My sister encouraged me to have it colored. I simply didn't care. I was struggling to stay alive and sane, and my hair was the least of my worries. I found myself short tempered, as all my emotions lay so close to the surface. As the weeks went on, I became even more worried as my husband retreated further and further from life. I had neighbors in the apartment building check on him and my two-year-old son throughout the evenings while I was at work. I took little care of myself, and it started taking its toll on me.

When people would ask how I was doing, I would tell them okay. I did not answer in an enthusiastic way, just a barely treading water kind of way. That is what I was doing– barely treading water. I could not participate in any grief groups because they usually met in the evening hours when I was at work. I also was not willing to leave my two-year-old son with my husband any more than necessary. My husband's depression was all consuming. I was so worried about Jim's safety.

I cannot recall where the suggestion came from, but we were given the name of a therapist who worked with grief victims. My husband and I went to see the therapist together. We just scratched the surface of our story in that first hour. We scheduled another appointment for the next week. When the time came to go, my husband refused to go with me. I had scheduled this counseling to try and get him some help and now he refused to go. I was furious! I went without him and soon found out that I deserved a little care and attention as well. It was a startling realization to me. I too deserved the time to grieve. I was not responsible for caring for everyone else.

Dear Kevin,

It has been three months since your death and the days are still full of agony. Will it ever end? Is my life to be a constant battle of will just to merely survive? People tell me that time will help. I am so tired of hearing that! I am barely alive anymore.

By now I should have been hearing the sound of wheels on my kitchen floor. They told me that was the first device they fit children with no legs in. It is a little basket that fastens around your tummy and it is attached to a platform with wheels on it so when you twist– like you did in Mommy's tummy; you can scoot about the room. I ache to hear that sound.

Kevin, where are you? I cannot stand the loneliness of the minutes without you. How am I going to make it now?

Love,
Mommy

Somehow in the midst of this despair, I struggled on. The days turned to weeks and the weeks to months. The hospital bills kept coming as a cruel reminder of my loss. In a desperate attempt, I called the hospital once again. The woman I reached listened patiently as I cried about how these reminders were tearing my heart out. I once again gave her all the information I could about payment. We set up a schedule and I never received another notice. There are angels in our presence. Those bills were just one more reminder I could no longer handle in my life and she was kind enough to understand and help me.

Dear Kevin,

I am so scared for tomorrow to come...it is only a few minutes away, but I am still so scared. I don't know if it is too much pain or just the awful realization that I have not held you for six whole months. Could it really be that long ago?

It seems like yesterday, so painfully clear to me. Or is it the pain of knowing I will never hold you again....

Love,

Mommy

Nine months after Kevin's death, we were on the move again. My husband had completed his training at seminary. I am not certain how that happened, it just did. He got a job offer, a call, at a pair of small rural congregations about 100 miles north of St. Paul in a rural area south of Brainerd, MN. I was ecstatic and yet apprehensive about the change. I had never been a city girl and hated living in the hustle of city life. Plus, this also meant for the first time in our marriage, I would not be the sole breadwinner. I looked at it as an opportunity for me to grieve without having to carry the load of responsibility on my shoulders. Yet, there would be no one there who knew Kevin.

The move was uneventful and we settled into a nice house in the country. I was scared and excited about the future all at the same time. When I look back on those days now, I realize how fragile my family was. I never wanted to let my son Jim, who was now nearly three, out of my sight. He never got dirty. I was always there to protect him. I smothered him with motherly attention and protection. When others tried to kindly point this out to me, I was immediately defensive. I had lost one son; I could not bear to lose another!

I recall the anniversary of Kevin's birthday. I had read many suggestions of having birthday cakes in honor of your lost child, planning a special day with the family, searching through the memories of your lost one. None of these worked for me. In the years to come I would have to find my own way. I remember a neighbor who lived one block down from the house we lived in when Kevin died. She told me of an older lady in her 90s that she knew. She had seven children and one of them died as a toddler. To that very day, still alive in her 90s, she would spend the entire birthday of that child, crying. She knew not to plan or expect anything of herself. She had given herself complete permission to grieve that day each year. When I first heard this, I was struck with the thought that I would never again be able to know joy. After time, I came to realize that this was her way of remembering and honoring her lost child. When all that remains to hold on to is your grief, you hold on with fervor!

Dear Kevin,

A little boy. Born just one year ago today. You changed my life in every way possible. I am so grateful I had you.

Happy first birthday my precious little one. Mommy loves you so very much. It has been such a hard day. I am so glad it is over.

Goodnight.

Love,

Mommy

The first anniversary of Kevin's death and funeral were not any easier than his birthday. Since they were only about a month apart, that whole two months of late summer were very difficult for me.

Dear Kevin,

I have been sitting here alone in the dark...crying and thinking. I hear your Daddy switching channels on the television, your brother Jim shifting in his bed to get comfortable. They are such familiar sounds mixed with the frogs' chirping; sounds I hear every night, but tonight I am so aware of the missing sound, you. I can only fill the void with my sobs of pain.

Oh Kevin, how I have dreaded this night. I am not sure I can make it through. I remember the moment when I pulled the tube out of your mouth and throat. It was then the machine stopped breathing for you. I rushed to pick you up. I wanted you to still be alive when I held you. I wanted you to die in my arms. And you did.

I had prayed for that moment to come– for you to be freed from the technical crap that made your little life hang on. Yet, I dreaded that moment as well.

I knew it was then I would have to say good-bye.

You are gone, And the sound of you in my house is missing. And it hurts...it hurts so very much.

Love,

Mommy

Dear Kevin,

Tonight the moon is full. It pierces the dark sky and the drifting clouds with a shining brilliance of a beacon. I know many people who are superstitious of a full moon. It is now my reference so I will not stumble on my way.

As I rest here in the quiet still of the night, the darkness envelops me and I recall how comforting the darkness is for me. It was not always this way. I can recall dreading the darkness of night. Now so much has changed. You died just over a year ago. You were only on this earth for five short weeks. My most precious moments with you were ours alone, in the stillness of the night. You would rest in my arms while I rocked you and sang to you. No one can imagine how I treasure those moments, and how because of them, the night is my friend.

Love,

Mommy

Chapter 4

The Courage to Live Again

There are no rules for the proper allotted time to grieve. I knew that then and I know it now. There is a difference in the grief when a parent loses a child. I didn't have a lifetime of memories to recall with fondness. All I had were a few short weeks filled with disappointments and a lifetime of wondering what my life would have been like if Kevin had lived.

Somehow in my mind I had told myself if I could survive that first year, I would be better. In some ways I was. The days were still difficult. I still smothered my remaining child with protection. I still shed many tears, but I also began to look to the future. In this painful process I learned much about myself and also about my faith. I was blessed with a faith life that helped me in these awful, dark days.

Dear Kevin,

I have very few regrets about your life and death and the way I handled it. I accept myself for what I could cope with then. I have learned so much and grown so. I will never repeat the words God never gives us more than

we can handle. It makes me so angry when I hear people throw out that platitude! I have never learned to handle your death. I hope that I have learned in some small way to accept it and try to learn to live with it. But never handle it.

Today, when I feel that familiar grief, I remind myself that God sits with me and cries. And when I need to get back into life, He gives me a warm embrace and a gentle nudge like a loving parent sending their precious child out into the world. And so I keep going, out into the world.

Love,
Mommy

It was after this first year that I made some decisions about my future. My husband and I had requested an autopsy be performed on Kevin's body immediately after his death. The results determined that his lung tissue was malformed in utero. His lungs never developed correctly to handle the exchange of oxygen into the blood stream. That explained why his heart valve remained open as the blood was shunted from one chamber of the heart to the other attempting to get oxygenated blood. At least this is how I understand it. They also did genetic testing and found no abnormalities that would suggest the absence of limbs and this strange lung tissue formation. We met and discussed this with Dr. Kurachek and consulted with a geneticist. They both felt confident that we would not have another child born like this. A *one-in-a-million mutation* was how they explained it. Dr. Kurachek suggested we give ourselves a year to grieve and heal and then think about trying for another baby if we like.

I guess those words planted in my mind, and I decided now that a year had come and gone, I could start looking to the future and the possibility of another baby. The idea terrified me, yet the experts had reassured me repeatedly that Kevin's disabilities were a rare mutation. It was not documented anywhere in medical history. Hence, the chances of it ever happening again were astronomical. We were reassured by the health of our first son, Jim. Certainly, we could have a healthy child again. My husband and I decided to try.

This decision was not an easy one. Deep down, I was terrified of the possible outcome. I was afraid to become pregnant again. I was also deeply worried that this would mean my son Kevin was insignificant to me. I had only grieved for him a year. I felt so much guilt about trying to move on with my life. But I did anyway. There was so much at stake. My marriage, my sanity, my chance for joy again.

Dear Kevin,

It has been just over a year since you died. There has not been a day that has gone by when I have forgotten you. Yet, at times, there is laughter again in my life. I feel so bad about that. Mommy does not want you to think I have stopped missing you. People ask me how many children I `have. How am I supposed to answer that?

I am so scared...scared that I have not grieved enough. Scared that I have not cried enough. When is it okay to start to live again?

The other day, your big brother and I were in the car together. He was looking at a book about Christmas. He turned the page to a picture of baby Jesus in the manger and told me it was a picture of you. I started to cry and told him, no, that was the baby Jesus. Not all babies are

named Kevin. I asked him if he remembered you and he said that he thought he did. He was unsure. Then he told me that Kevin was with Jesus. I told him that was right.

"I think Jesus was sad when Kevin died Mom," he said.

"Yes," I replied, through a veil of tears. "I think Jesus was sad."

We were both silent for a while. Then, looking into the clouds, your three-year-old brother said, " I think Jesus will kiss Kevin goodnight Mommy."

"Yes," I replied. "I think so."

God, how my heart aches for you, my little boy.

Love,

Mommy

So the decision was made and I soon found out I was pregnant again. Looking back, I now notice that there is a period of a few months without journal entries. I felt so guilty about looking to the future without my son, I could not face writing about my newfound fears.

Dear Kevin,

And now what? I am carrying your little brother or sister in my womb. I feel the movements, kicks I pray. I ache in my heart for you and yet I ache for the promise of this new little life. Then I feel that I am abandoning your memory as I think of this new little one. Oh Kevin, is there no end to this pain?

Sometimes I feel myself detaching from this new life. I am so afraid I will lose him or her. Why bother to dream of what could be?

I feel so frail and frightened. I feel like the child. Please watch over Mommy. I love you.

Love,
Mommy

When I learned I was pregnant again, I took all the medical data with me that I had compiled about Kevin and his short life with me. I was immediately referred to an OB/GYN instead of a family practice doctor. She listened to my story and looked over the reports and data I provided. She suggested a rigorous schedule of ultrasound tests and blood tests to insure we would know what was coming. She insisted this was to reassure me that everything would be normal in the pregnancy.

My new doctor scheduled a specialized ultrasound test called a Level II Ultrasound when I was nineteen weeks pregnant. My husband and I had to drive over 100 miles to a prenatal specialist in Minneapolis for the test. I was so scared. The test was conducted in the hospital next to Minneapolis Children's Hospital where Kevin died. I could feel the tension in my chest as we approached the buildings.

We met with the specialist for a few minutes and then went into the examining room for the ultrasound. The technician was kind and patient as the test began. She showed me the head and the arms of our new little one. I could not believe the joy I felt when I saw that baby's arms and hands. Then she went on to the legs. And she kept going over and over the same spot. As the baby twisted, she tried again. I knew something was wrong. She called in another technician who looked. I kept asking what was wrong. What did they see? They tried to reassure me, but I knew they were worried. Finally, the specialist came into the room. He started by asking us if we wanted to know what sex *she* was. I answered that I guess he just told us. I was so happy to have a little girl! He went methodically through the ultrasound test showing us the baby's head and arms and hands. He even looked at the internal organs and found them to be normal for this age.

Then the bomb dropped. My baby did not have normal lower extremities. My little girl did not have fully developed legs. At this point, the specialist was not sure if it was one leg or both, as he could not get a clear enough view of the second leg. There was no foot on the one leg and it looked like one of the lower calf bones was missing as well. He tried to reassure me, telling me that the rest of her looked normal. And then it occurred to me why my doctor had insisted we do this test before twenty weeks. The specialist explained there were certain options still available if we wanted to terminate the pregnancy. I immediately responded, "No!" I had her name picked out already– Jill. She was already my daughter, despite my attempts to remain detached from this life growing inside of me.

When my husband and I got home, there was a list of phone calls to make. I cannot recall how many or to whom exactly, but there was a list. People were shocked and bewildered, much the same as we had been. How could this happen again? Certainly, the baby's lungs would be normal. A lot of people live very full lives with a disability. One missing leg is not that bad.

We went back to the same specialist a month later for another ultrasound. I hoped for the same results. There was more bad news. This time they got a clearer picture. It was confirmed that Jill had disabilities on both legs. They could see thighbones and the rest was absent. There appeared to be no bone or muscle structure past the thigh. Once again, they reassured us that her internal organs appeared normal. I was not convinced.

Dear Kevin,

People ask me if it is better to know...now that we know your sister will not be born in perfect health. I am not sure. I keep praying that the doctors have not missed anything. I am so scared...scared that I will not be able to handle the challenges Jill may have.

I feel like a failure as a mother. I have failed to produce a healthy child. Isn't that what mothers are supposed to do?

You and your sister were in my womb. I have to take some responsibility for your death and her handicaps. I feel so cheated. And then someone makes a comment about handicapped children and how it is the parents who have the problem! Take a walk in my shoes! Then you can tell me how it feels to be cheated out of a healthy child.

I am so lonely and so tired of struggles and pain. I keep trying to have faith, whatever that means. I feel like I am faking my whole self sometimes. I cannot let people see how devastated I am. What would they think? I am a pastor's wife after all. I must have faith. Then I feel a kick and I wonder if it is a leg. Could they be wrong? I am so overwhelmed.

I try to remember that all I need to worry about is today. But today has been so sad and I know tomorrow will be as well– and I cannot wait for it to end.

Love,
Mommy

I was surrounded by people who tried to shore me up with their prayers and good wishes. I had no one close to me that had lived through my ordeal with losing Kevin. I was in a new home and here I sat, a pastor's wife, putting on a face of faith. I did not use my family of origin as I could have. They were all hurting so much. I could not bear their pain on top of my own and I felt guilty and shameful for bringing another sorrow into their lives.

There were many who assured me that the doctors are often wrong about these things. Well-meaning people told me they were certain God would give this new baby legs before it was born. Like she would sprout complete limbs in the last months in utero. I know they were only trying to help, but it was such a lonely time for me.

When I saw another pregnant woman in the store or on the street, I couldn't help but wonder if she knew if her baby was healthy. Could she tell that my baby wasn't? What had I done wrong this time? The genetic experts had already told me this could never happen again. One in a million, they said. Here I was facing those same fears again. I just kept praying that she would have normal lung tissue and she would live. It was going to be a long three months waiting to find out.

Chapter 5

The Nightmare Returns

I didn't have three months to wait. One evening in March, just two days after my birthday, I lay down on the couch after putting my oldest son to bed. I fell asleep somewhere around 9 P.M. and woke with a start just after 10 P.M. I got up quickly and ran to the bathroom. It was that familiar pressure again. My water broke. I was only thirty weeks along in my pregnancy, so I knew this was not good news. I called the hospital and told them we were coming. They told me to hurry. I wasn't in that much of a hurry because it had taken Kevin a long time to be born after my water broke. We arranged for the neighbor to come and stay with our son. My husband and I drove to the hospital in Brainerd, thirty miles north of our home. I was a little uncomfortable, but not feeling pain, except the gut wrenching realization that I might be losing this child.

The hospital was much more concerned about the developments than I was. My doctor suggested that I be transferred to a major hospital in Minneapolis. This was 130 miles south of where I was. She insisted they would be better able to postpone the premature delivery of my baby. I dreaded going back to this hospital that was adjacent to Children's Hospital where Kevin died. I cried, trying to convince her to take care of me there. She refused. I started feeling back pain, and some slight contractions as well. She recommended a helicopter take me, but after some medication seemed to ease the pain, we opted for an ambulance ride.

It was a long, awful ride. A nurse rode with me in the back and tried to help, but the ride made my back labor much worse. It seemed to take forever and I found myself drifting in my thoughts. My husband had driven home and picked up our son, Jim. I have no idea what he said to that little boy as he whisked him out of his bed and drove to Minneapolis. That must have been an awful ride as well.

I recall very little from that night after that except that I was losing a great deal of fluid and blood. The doctors put me on IVs with heavy doses of magnesium that was designed to slow the contractions. It made me lose my sense of reality. I remember my parents coming into the room, but only faintly. They had driven to the hospital to take my three-year-old son home with them.

There was a nurse who cared for me those first few days. She was reassuring and patient. I asked her if I was going to be able to keep this baby. She told me she had never seen someone lose as much fluid as I had and still not deliver. When I was transferred to the ante-partum ward, she requested to be my nurse. The ante-partum ward of the hospital is designed solely for women in some form of premature labor. (I referred to it, as the *let's not have a baby today* ward.) Her name was Elaine. She was an angel God sent to me.

I was not a good patient. Just the word patient is not an adjective anyone who knows me would use to describe me. I insisted that I go home. She and the doctors told me no. I kept thinking over and over, how am I going to stay in this hospital bed for the next ten weeks? Elaine would smile and ask me to try to make it through this one day. "Every day you keep that baby in your womb is so important," she said. "Try to make it just through today." So I did.

It took me about one weeks stay in the hospital before I resigned myself to keeping that baby in my womb no matter what the cost. I took delight in little freedoms. After the first week, I was allowed to walk five steps to the shower every other day. I took my trusty IV pole with me. It was a special delight to walk those few steps and sit upright in a chair. I was also awarded a commode immediately adjacent to my bed. No more bedpans after that first week. Oh, the little pleasures we enjoy!

I made a chart of the days with Jill's weeks of gestation on it. I drew big stars when we would reach another complete week. The doctor had set a goal of thirty-six weeks gestation. I was already at thirty-one weeks. It seemed like a long way off, but I could do it if it would save my daughter's life.

I was blessed with a sister and a former college roommate who visited almost daily. They helped to cheer me and keep me sane.

My husband was struggling with his own losses and needs at this time, so his mother went to stay with him and our son while I was hospitalized. I wrote out lists of what was necessary to do to take care of the house and his job. He brought the mail and the checkbook to me so I could handle the bills. I told him if it was too difficult to drive down to see me frequently, he should come just once a week.

I felt I had to be strong. I denied my own needs once again and put on a front.

Because of this, I saw my husband and three-year-old son once a week. They would come to visit on Sunday afternoons and stay for about an hour each time. It was an awful time. By then, my marriage was already shaky and his visits didn't help.

When my roommates' spouses visited, they laid in bed and held them. They spoke words of reassurance and love. My husband would bring the Sunday paper with him and read it. When I would try to talk with him, he would become frustrated at my interruption. When I asked him to lie on the bed with me, he refused, saying he would worry about my IV or the mess it would make if my womb would leak. Instead of being the reassuring voice for me, I was the voice for him.

More than anything, I craved my moments with my little son, Jim. We had been inseparable, and we missed each other terribly. I would ask him to climb up into my arms, but he wouldn't stay long because my husband would tell him to get down, as he was concerned about bumping into my IV. I could not reassure my son that it was okay– that he could stay with me on that bed. I was so hurt.

When my husband finished reading the Sunday paper, they would leave. It tore my heart up to see my little boy walk out the door. "Are you really sick Mommy?" he would ask. He just did not understand. I ached to jump out of that bed and go home with him.

Dear Kevin,

The sky is so beautiful tonight, blue, orange and pink. I can see it clearly. I am in the hospital on the fifth floor.

Your daddy remembered to bring this journal with him today. Now I can write to you.

My membranes have ruptured. And here I lie in this bed. I have been here for twelve days now, twelve long days without seeing your big brother but a couple of stolen minutes. The baby is thirty- two weeks along now. They want me to try and hold on as long as I can. So I stay in bed and pass the time. One of the women across the ward was here twenty-six days and her baby died. Oh God, how it brought back so much pain from when I lost you.

I am so afraid this little one will die too. Where can I bury her? I cannot bear to go to visit two different cemeteries to place flowers on my children's graves.

It is almost completely dark now. That ís how my heart feels too. I try to keep up my hope, my faith. I just cannot lose her, like I lost you.

Love,
Mommy

I have a new appreciation for what life must be like in a nursing home. I was taken care of by my nurses. I was restricted in my activity. I had no idea what day it was most of the time. And time dragged on as I prayed for night to come so another day could be marked off the chart. And then I would lie in that bed. I was not allowed to wear underwear for fear of infection, and the fluid would leak out of my womb and trickle between my legs. It was nearly impossible to sleep. So I would lay there in the dark and sob as quietly as I could so as not to disturb whatever roommate I might have. They came and went. I couldn't keep track of them. Their stays were short, and I was just stuck there for an eternity!

Dear Kevin,

It is finally dark now. I have been waiting for the darkness to fall. I only hope I can sleep tonight. I am so tired of this incontinent feeling.

I have been here sixteen days now. I am so torn between wanting the hell out of this bed and knowing I have to stay here for this baby.

I am so scared...and lonely...and tired. The doctor wants me to wait another three weeks and then he will let me deliver. Three more weeks, twenty-one days. I don't think I can make it. I wish I was stronger or more patient or something.

Please God; do not let my little Jill die too. I know she will not be perfect in health, but I love her so much already. It is your will. I must follow it, no matter what happens. I just am not sure I will be able to live, to draw another breath if she leaves me too.

Please God, am I asking too much?

Love,

Mommy

I made it a few more days. On the twenty-fourth day of my stay, the gestational age of thirty-four weeks for my little girl; I woke up early in the morning to labor pains. I had not had any of them for over three weeks. I immediately called the nurse telling her they were about twelve minutes apart. More medications were ordered to try to stop the contractions. I called my husband. It was 7 A.M. on a Sunday morning. He had two church services to perform. I told him to go ahead and preach his sermons. Once again, I was tough. I called my sister, who was a cardiac nurse at that time and I called my angel nurse, Elaine. She came in on her day off to be with me.

About 9A.M., they decided the medications were not working and I was going to have a baby. My contractions were still five minutes apart so I went back to the delivery ward of the hospital where I had first been admitted. The monitor on my belly registered that the baby struggled during contractions. I was scared. I felt the urge to push and told the nurse so. The delivery nurse had just checked me. Elaine insisted she check again. I was fully dilated, having gone from four to complete in less than five minutes. I was rushed to the delivery room. With one familiar push, my daughter was born. They held up my little four– pound– seven– ounce girl for me to see for a split second and then the team assembled around her plastic confinement. Jill cried only for a short second and then she opened her eyes when I spoke to her. That was the only time my daughter looked at me. The only time I saw her eyes. The only time.

The doctor who delivered Jill told me they would take her to Children's Hospital next door. He felt confident that she was breathing on her own, but that she might need oxygen due to her prematurity. She was six weeks early. My sister went with me to the recovery room where they insisted I eat something before I went to see my baby. My sister ate a couple bites of the sandwich and we threw the rest in the trash, covering the food strategically with the papers that were already there. I drank some juice and got into the wheelchair. I wanted to walk. I wanted to get up and walk so bad, but the people around me convinced me that the walk through the long tunnel that stretched over a city block connecting the hospitals might be a bit much after spending the last twenty-four days in bed and delivering a baby less than an hour before. I knew they were right, but I was going to see my daughter. It was going to take a lot more than a couple of well-meaning nurses to stop me!

When my sister wheeled me into the doors of the Neonatal Intensive Care Unit, I felt a familiar crushing pain in my chest. There was my baby girl– on oxygen. I met her doctor and talked to him briefly. He asked me if he could consult with Kevin's doctor since there might be some similarities. I told him I wished he would.

I could not get enough of my precious Jill. She had sandy brown curls all over her tiny head. She weighed just over four pounds, but was a giant compared to the other babies in that unit. She had the longest fingers of any baby I have seen. I immediately started daydreaming about her playing the piano for me. I must have been there a while. My husband and son came in too. They missed her delivery by two hours.

The doctor and nurses all spoke words of reassurance. I tried to share their hope. They kept suggesting I go back to my room to lie down. After all, they kept saying, you just had a baby! I did not want to leave, but they kept insisting. They wheeled me back to the ward only to find they had given my familiar room to a new patient. I had a few minutes of joy as we called friends and family telling them the good news. Jill was born and breathing on her own! While I was in the bathroom, the phone rang. As soon as the voice on the other end started talking, I knew my joy was over.

Dear Kevin,

They told me she was doing well. They made me leave! I did not want to leave her! All my worst fears are being realized. Jill's on a respirator now. It doesn't look like she will live. Twenty-four days I stayed in this hospital. For what? How much more can my heart take?

She just can't die. I can't do this again. God, please don't make me live this nightmare again!

Love,

Mommy

While I had returned to the ward that had been my home for the last twenty-four days, to get that rest everyone insisted I needed, my daughter had gone into respiratory arrest. They had connected her to a respirator and now she was dependent on a machine for her life. I knew it was the beginning of the end.

Chapter 6
Another Good-bye

I insisted on going to see Jill right away. Now all the phone calls of joy we had made were for naught. The experts tried to reassure me this might be a temporary setback. I had little faith in their false sense of hope. I remember vividly walking into the NICU on the afternoon of her birth. I heard the familiar rhythm of the respirator and watched the false rise of her little chest and stomach. Already, I could see the air collecting in her tummy as the machine breathed for her lifeless body. It was horrific.

We met in the NICU with Dr. Kurachek, the pulmonary specialist that had cared for Kevin just twenty months ago. To say he was sympathetic would not begin to describe the level of emotion I felt from that man. He sat down beside me and hung his head. The only words he could say were, "I can't believe we are here doing this again. I am so sorry." He must have repeated those words several times because they rang in my head for days and months to come. He knew there was little hope. He knew my daughter's fate, just as I did.

Dear Jill,

Here we go again. How I prayed and feared this day would come. But here it is. You are so beautiful, my little one. They moved the oxygen sensor off of your hand to your little funny-shaped leg. I don't know what to call it. I don't care about your little legs, my darling; I still think you are the most beautiful little baby I have ever seen. I keep thinking about funerals and burials. I cannot seem to keep my mind from wandering to those thoughts. I feel like it is inevitable, your death. I am afraid I have little faith left for miracles. I have prayed too long for one. It doesn't look like I am going to get one now either.

They tried to lay you on your right side. You did not like that, neither did Kevin. It haunts me how much you remind me of Kevin.

Where will we bury you? What do I dress you in for your coffin? Is there any hope at all for you? Is it my fault for not having enough faith?

I know I will never hear you cry, or look into your eyes again. And what about your big brother? He is only three years old and so many awful experiences to live with.

We were all so excited. They told us you were doing so well. I waited for the delivery and felt your shoulders and arms come out of my body. I felt those little legs too. I was not scared of how you looked when you were born. I knew your legs would be different than most babies. I just wanted to keep you with me.

But you are not going to stay. You are going to heaven to be with your brother Kevin and with Jesus. This life is not worth staying here for.

Love,

Mommy

I had to walk from the ward to an elevator, ride down to the basement, and then walk an underground tunnel about one block long, taking the elevator in Children's Hospital to the NICU ward. I had not walked for twenty-four days until this day, but I was getting a lot of walking in now. The nurses insisted I push a wheelchair in front of me. I was not riding anymore! As I walked back from seeing my Jill that evening, a drop of blood from my womb dropped onto the floor. I stopped and looked at it. I was a little embarrassed as there was another couple with my husband and me. We had nothing to clean it with. Later when we made the return trip back to the NICU ward, we noted the blood was still there. It was dried and crusted to the floor. We decided it was symbolic. It was how my heart felt, full of old pain and bleeding with even more, going unnoticed by the world as it hurried by.

When I returned to the ward where I had been, the nurses had kindly moved me back to my familiar room. I guess they thought it would be a small comfort and it was. They arranged for the other bed in my room to be empty and allowed my husband to stay there. They offered me medication to help me sleep. I took the pills and gave them to my husband. I did not want to sleep. I wanted to be at my daughter's side. Everyone kept insisting I go back to my bed and rest. I started writing in Kevin's journal. This time it was letters to Jill.

I did drift for a few hours and got up in the middle of the night and decided to go to see Jill by myself. I started to walk and got as far as the nurse's station before they stopped me. I guess they were afraid I was a little weak to be moving around so much. They did not want me to go alone on that walk, but they soon found out that no was not an acceptable answer for me. I am not sure why well-meaning people push away loved ones from someone who is dying. They were the final precious moments of Jill's life and they wanted me to detach from it. Maybe it makes their impossible job easier to handle. I don't know. I finally convinced the nurses I was going whether they had orders to stop me or not.

They did talk me into taking a wheelchair in case I got tired, and I agreed. There was something so peaceful about the hospital that night. When I walked into the NICU ward, they were a bit surprised to see me. But I held my daughter's hand and talked to her when no one else was around. I had her all to myself. It was like the quiet nights I had spent alone with my Kevin. This one was sterile and foreign, but it was still just my tiny daughter and I, together.

I left when the sun was up and made the journey back to my ward in the other hospital. The bloodstain on the tunnel floor was gone. It would be like that in the grieving too, others would stop and pause, say a word of sympathy for us and then it would be over– an afterthought. I knew it was coming.

I went back to my room and took a shower. My husband was awake now. I gathered my things together. I packed everything in my room. It was ready to go. We were going to meet with Jill's doctor at 10 A.M. I knew what this meeting meant. I took along my camera, a little dress Jill had gotten from my nurse friend, Elaine, a scissors and envelope, a small comb, a piece of paper, and an ink pad. When I walked in with my little *kit* of wares, the social worker and chaplain looked at me with a bit of surprise. I answered them with confidence, "I have done this before. I am prepared."

The meeting with the doctor was as I suspected. He agreed that the tests showed that Jill was never going to breathe on her own. Her lungs must also have abnormal tissue as Kevin's had. We could make a decision to discontinue life support. We agreed. It was not an easy decision, but it was a simple one. I knew what had to happen and at least this time I was not battling with a team of professionals who wanted a voice in the future of my child.

They gave us a small private room to go to. I helped wash the Benzion Tincture (the orangish brown medicine they use in hospitals before they start an IV or sew stitches) from all her IV spots. The nurse helped me make ink prints of her hands. And once again, I pulled the tube from her mouth, freeing another child from artificial life. I dressed her in her new little dress. I combed her hair. I wrapped her in a little blanket and carried her to the room they had set up for us. It was just the four of us, my husband and I, and our two children. We took some pictures. We cut a lock of her hair and placed it in the envelope. We cried and moaned, and said our good-byes as best we could. The nurse checked in periodically and listened for a heartbeat with the stethoscope. I didn't care what time they put on her death certificate. I had to hold my daughter, even if it was only for a few moments. Everyone else left and I stayed with her for a while. I wasn't ready to give her up. I like to think she died in my arms, much the same as her brother had less than two years ago.

Dear Jill,

I am not sure I quite believe it, but you are gone now. You have been dead for nearly twelve hours. I am home again, finally. There sits your little room all decorated for you. I am so glad I did not put up your crib. It would have been just another painful reminder– that empty crib again.

I drove the 100 miles home. I insisted on it. I just wanted to feel some sense of control in my life. I had laid in that hospital and listened to what the medical professionals told me to do. I was not perfect, but I tried so very hard to be good. I just kept hoping they could save you. And now you are gone. Gone forever.

I just wanted to see your first tooth, your first steps. I wanted to braid your hair, buy you a new dress. They are all dreams now. I had you for two days. And now once again, I have an empty womb and empty arms. I have nothing.

Love,

Mommy

Jill died on a Tuesday morning and we set the funeral for Friday morning. There was much to be done. I once again shifted into task mode and went feverishly around my house, cleaning it. The funeral would be held at one of the churches where my husband was pastor and the reception would be at our home. I raked the yard and did anything I could to stay busy. The phone rang incessantly. I did not bother to pick it up. My husband did the talking and crying. I kept moving. I was afraid if I stopped, I would fall apart.

We made arrangements at the funeral home and found, much to our comfort, that there was indeed just enough room to bury Jill next to her brother Kevin. At least it was only one cemetery to visit.

The funeral home director showed us the variety of caskets from the gold gilded model to the insulated cooler used for your sodas or beer. We chose one in the middle.

The next morning I drove the thirty miles to the nearest shopping mall, by myself. It had been four days since I had a baby, and I had been confined to my bed for some time prior to that. It was probably not a smart decision, but I had no options in my mind. My husband didn't want to go, and I had to get Jill something to wear for her funeral. I went to all the major stores looking for preemie-sized clothing. None of them had any, making this task even more difficult. The store clerks would immediately start asking questions about my baby. My swollen belly made it obvious I had just had a baby. I cried and told them I was shopping for her funeral. Then I would turn away without looking for an expression on their faces. I did have the one dress she had received as a gift. It fit her, but I could not part with it. I had so little to remember her by. The dress had a stain on the collar from some Tincture of Benzoin we must not have completely washed off. That was how Jill smelled. The dress smelled like my baby girl. I could not give it up.

I finally walked into a toy store and found Cabbage Patch Kids and accessories. The clerk was very patient and understanding. She helped me decide upon a little white dress with multicolored hearts. There was a matching bonnet as well. I bought the outfit and dropped it off at the funeral home. I drove away. Then I stopped at the side of the road, got out of my car, and screamed and howled with all my might. I hurt in every part of my body. I was going to bury my daughter, my Jill. It was going to happen.

Dear Jill,

Today is the day. The day of your funeral. My little girl's funeral. What an event. Mommy is so sad and tired of having funerals for her babies. That's all I have, funerals and boxes in the closet holding a few mementos.

My chest is so sore. Seems my milk came in yesterday and my breasts are so swollen. I still look pregnant. I have nothing to wear. I cannot wear a maternity dress.

Those are designed for mothers who are in joyful anticipation. They are not for sad mommies who are burying their little ones.

It is an awful day. Mommy is so very sad.

Love,

Mommy

Once again the funeral was a blur. My husband and I planned a short visitation before the funeral. Many people came to offer their support. We planned the funeral the same as Kevin's. We asked the same ministers to participate. We had the same solo. We sang, "Jesus Loves Me" as a hymn instead of "Children of the Heavenly Father". I remember my niece who, at the time, had just turned three. She looked at Jill in that casket and asked her mom, "Who's doll is that?" Jill did look like a little doll lying in that casket. She was so beautiful. And she was at peace. Everyone came over to our house for fellowship after the funeral and ate. It was wonderful and awful at the same time. I knew when they were all around me that I would be fine, but I knew there would be so many days ahead with no one there. I knew I was not okay.

Our little family drove the next day into Wisconsin where we had a small committal service at the cemetery where Jill was to be buried. Once again, there was a reception at the church where people from our former community expressed their love and sympathy. I guess you could say we had a great deal of ritual for her leaving this world. I needed that. I needed others to see her and touch her, if they liked. She had to be a real person to them. It was so important to me.

Chapter 7

And Where the Hell Did God Go?

After Kevin died, I was in a state of shock and disbelief. I felt all those familiar stages of grief. I was angry, I bargained with God, and I finally came to some sort of acceptance. This time was different. I had accepted it as God's will when Kevin died. It was not easy, but I had an understanding of His omnipotence. Who was I to question that? Do not misunderstand me. I was still angry about what had happened, but my grief was more filled with sadness than anything else.

Now Jill had died. I prayed before conceiving her to be shown the right direction. Everyone around me in my life at the time had been reassuring, even the medical experts. I truly felt that God wanted me to try again. I took a leap of faith, and then the bombshells began to drop. First it was the ultrasound tests, one after another filling me with more doubt and questions. Then it was premature labor with my membranes rupturing at thirty weeks gestation. This was followed by three and a half weeks in bed, all the while being reassured by caring friends, family, and professionals. Then came the day of her birth and the positive signs. I was overjoyed, until the final bomb dropped and shattered all my hope for joy again.

After the funeral and burial came those lonely days of putting away baby things, paying hospital bills, answering the phone, and telling the whole story once again. The rest of the world returned to normal, and my world collapsed. I was so sad. And then I got angry, so very angry. I was angry at everyone, everything, but mostly at God. If He is omnipotent, all-powerful, just what the hell did he think he was pulling in my life? Others had been granted miracles. Why not me? This anger manifested itself in so many ways. I did not take care of myself. I would eat nothing for days and then gorge myself afterwards. I would try to relive over and over again in my mind what I could have done differently. The autopsy report for Jill showed the same strangely formed lung tissue as Kevin's. There were no answers.

Dear Jill,

Last night I held your little Pooh Bear. It was the same size as you. I played the music just like your big brother Jim did for you in the hospital. I cuddled that bear and held it so tight and cried. I cried so very hard I thought I might break in two. There is nothing more to say except that Mommy is so sad.

Love,
Mommy

Painful reminders were everywhere. Mother's Day.

Dear Jill,

Mother's Day is over. I am so glad, so relieved. I do not feel like a good mother. Mothers Day is just another reminder of the fact that I have three children but the world only sees one. How am I supposed to answer people when they ask me how many children I have?

I miss you so. I prayed and prayed. I feel so cheated. It was supposed to be my turn. They told me it was going to be okay. Everyone kept telling me it was going to be okay. They denied me the feelings of fear so I buried them deep down and felt guilty for doubting God. Now tell me who was right?

My heart is in a million pieces. It will never be whole again. Only a miracle could do that. And I don't believe in them, not anymore.

Love,

Mommy

Mothers are supposed to protect their children. I couldn't even protect my children when they were in my womb. People asked if there was anything I was exposed to. It had to be something I did. I got very tired of repeating that there was no explanation. Once again, the world is much more comfortable with explainable tragedies. Then we can all distance ourselves from them. It will never happen to me.

I have a friend who has two boys and her last baby, a girl, was born prematurely. She died at birth. She still grieves that her last baby was her failure as a mother. We put so much emphasis on women to be mothers. Woe to us who fall short of those expectations. That's exactly how I felt. One minute I was overcome by the sense of my failure as a mother and the next I was so angry at God I could not bear my own rage.

Many people tried to tell me it was not okay to be angry with God. I had no other choice. I was so full of anger. I couldn't direct it at my family. That would be devastating to them. I couldn't direct it at the doctors, clearly they were dumfounded by my children's conditions. I couldn't direct it at myself, because when I did, I found myself in a state of depression teetering on suicide. The only safe place to direct my anger was at God. I never stopped believing in Him. I just got damn angry. When people would question my feelings, I would remind them that even Jesus got angry with His Father. I was secure enough in my faith that somehow God would forgive me. He knew how terribly my heart ached. He had to understand that.

Dear Jill,

I just woke up. The birds are singing. I like to wake up that way. I have been so sad lately. I lost the checkbook yesterday. It was the final straw. I feel so out of control. I go through this life, just going through the motions. I feel dizzy, disorganized. I forget everything. It is such a struggle just to make it through the day and keep on living. I am so tired.

I have been thinking an awful lot about suicide. I would be with you and Kevin. Babies need their mommy. I want so badly to be your mommy. I have imagined all the different ways I could kill myself. But I cannot leave your big brother Jim alone. So I have decided on a car accident, it is certain to be final, it is the answer. I could not bear to live if Jim would die without me.

How am I supposed to live? How am I supposed to live?

Love,

Mommy

And then sometimes I thought I was starting to heal. But the healing and glimpses of hope were always tainted with my grief.

Dear Jill,

It is a beautiful morning. I have so much planned for today. I try to keep as busy as I can. It helps to make the day go quickly. I am so grateful for mornings like this when I need to jump into the day. It's the still of the quiet morning and evening that remind me of my emptiness. Kevin and I shared quiet mornings and evenings. You and I never got that special time. I miss you so very much my sweet little girl.

Love,
Mommy

One of the things I learned through these years is that grieving is not a static event. It seems to ebb and flow. Just as I thought I was really getting better, something would strike me so painfully hard I could scarcely breathe, let alone function. I would see a newborn baby girl. I would walk by the infant department in a clothing store. It would not take much to trigger those feelings and I would be forced to stuff them down deep inside of me so I could continue living. It may sound strange, but at those moments I had no desire to continue living. I wanted all of it to stop. I wanted life to stop.

Dear Jill,

I miss you so. I feel so all alone. I watch your big brother sleeping and he is holding his favorite toy. I think how much I ache to hold you in my arms, just like that.

People do not understand how lonely and sad I am. It has been three months and I get the feeling they want me to be all better. The other day I was shopping with someone. She stopped to look at baby clothes. I was right there! I got hurt and angry and walked away. She got angry with me and said it was not fair, as she was excited about this baby soon to be born in her family. I told her I was sorry, but it just hurt too much. I cannot do it! She never apologized or said anything.

Why do I have to be the one to be understanding? She tells me it is unfair for me to not allow her to be happy. What is fair anymore?

Someone tell me what is fair in this world? I certainly cannot tell anymore.

I am so alone.

Love,

Mommy

We all grieve differently. When my son Kevin died, I plunged into my grief, but not too far. Someone needed to keep functioning. My husband was acutely depressed. He barely functioned. I knew that after Jill died, it would not be any better. I was right. It was much worse. There were days he barely got out of bed. He slept during the day and would stay up at night watching mindless television shows. I urged him to get some professional help, but he resisted. I couldn't tell anyone how poorly we were doing. He was a pastor. We needed to be the role model of faith and perseverance. I started burying my feelings and trying to put on that stoic appearance. I pretended I was handling the whole thing very well. I consistently told people I was doing okay. In other words, I lied a lot.

My former college roommate told me much later that I was so reassuring to her; she decided I was going to be just fine. I just would not allow myself to burden others with my pain. And so I was alone. I desperately wanted someone to see through my mask. No one did. If they did, they never said so.

I must have been convincing in my reassurance, my cover. I tried attending local meetings of grief support groups. After the first meeting, the leaders asked me to come back so I would be there to offer support for others who had lost babies. I did not want to offer help to someone else. I wanted someone to offer it to me. I attended a different meeting and the leader pointed out to me that I seemed angry and had better move on. If I was angry before, now I was really angry. I never went back to either group.

I did not lean on my extended family. I saw the grief in their eyes and hearts and I felt responsible for hurting them so. I could not burden them with my problems. I continued to search for my sanity in other people and places.

It was during these months that my family awaited the birth of my sister's baby. This baby was due in August, just four months after my daughter died. My feelings were so torn. I was caught between feeling happy for my sister and her family and the rage over the loss of my precious little one.

Dear Jill,

Your aunt is due to have her baby tomorrow. I dread the news. I hope and pray it is a boy. I know that sounds terrible, but I keep telling myself if it is a boy, I will handle it easier. I just miss you so much. I cannot share this with anyone. It is too evil and selfish.

Love,
Mommy

And then the baby was born. I was relieved that everything was okay and angry that I could not know that same joy in my life. It was awful to be in that position. I still look at that boy and try to imagine my little girl being that same age. Somehow, I cannot picture her as a growing child. She is still my baby in my mind and heart. I suppose that is how she will always be to me.

Dear Jill and Kevin,

Hope it is okay that I write to you together.

It happened. Your aunt had a baby boy. He has ten fingers and ten toes and a head full of dark hair. It seems like an eternity since your big brother was born healthy like that. I am glad he is a boy. I know that is terrible of me to say. I just know I could not shop for anything in the little girls section. Everyone is so happy for them. I am too, but I cannot shake the envy in my heart. Why not me?

Love,
Mommy

The world kept moving, even as my grief left me standing still in time. I soon found out that although I thought I had grieved the loss of Kevin, Jill's death made all those feelings come back. I would feel guilt for not grieving their deaths in the same way. Face it, I felt guilt over everything. I was their mother. I allowed this to happen. Somehow it had to be my fault. Parents protect their children.

I was blessed in the fact that I could sleep at night. Many people who suffer in their grief do not get that respite. I tried my best to wear myself out physically during the day so I could sleep. It helped. But then the dreams would come. I had recurring dreams of my children being born healthy only to realize when I woke, that they were dead. I would sometimes race to the bedroom looking for them as soon as

I woke up. I kept hoping I was wrong, that they were still alive somehow. It was a cruel price to pay for the hours of sleep I got.

Dear Jill and Kevin,

I just woke up. I am so grateful for the morning. I had this dream last night that I went to the doctor and she told me I was pregnant again. I could not believe it. I went home and the next day, I started bleeding. I was having a miscarriage. Now that doctor who told me it was remarkable that I could carry Kevin to term was being justified. It was like someone was punishing me. I could not have even one full day of joy! When I woke up, I found my period had started. Will the nightmares ever end?

Love,
Mommy

I was stuck in my anger for quite a while. When Kevin died, I had some anger, but it was manageable. When Jill died, I was downright furious with the world and God. I had lived through the grieving of one child. Throughout that time I felt alone. My husband and I did not share our grief. I had not felt support from him during that time.

As soon as I learned that Jill was going to heaven, I knew I was in for a long road. There were moments where I found glimpses of hope or joy, but then I would feel guilt for them because it meant I was moving on. It happened one morning, five months after Jill died, that I found a metaphor for my struggle while sitting on my front steps.

Dear Jill and Kevin,

Such a cloudy morning; it sprinkled all morning and now it is sunny and warm. Strange how quickly a day can change. I am sitting on the front step writing to you and soaking up some of that sunshine. A small black bug started crawling up the steps and onto my foot. I flicked it way with my pen. He fell on his back and now he is struggling. His legs are kicking frantically– desperately trying to get upright again.

I nudged him gently so he would return to upright again and watched him rush around here and there, traveling in frantic circles in every direction. He made no sense toward any destination. When he started his crawl toward me he seemed deliberate and sure. Now he seemed confused and traumatized; his comfortable existence was so rudely disrupted. Finally, he scampered off into the grass out of my sight.

It is crazy how an insect can touch my heart so. I cannot help but wonder if that is what I am. I was on my path, sure of my destination in this life. Then I loved and lost the two of you. Now, I feel like someone threw me off course. I am on my back, kicking frantically to find some sense...to hold on to this life. I kicked and twisted with all my might...to get upright. After you died, Kevin, I thought I was okay. Then it happened again and I lost you, Jill. Now I am really lost. I cannot seem to find my path. I am not even sure if I want the same path. I am going around in circles, dazed and confused. I have wandered into the tall grass of this life where everyone and everything goes on as normal, without me.

And my pain and confusion is out of their sight. My grief is gone from their memory.

Love,

Mommy

I was so wrapped in my own pain that it was difficult to care for others. I made my primary focus my one remaining son, Jim. I tried to make his life as normal as I could, although I knew it was not. He witnessed his mother full of rage and sorrow. He witnessed his father retreating into depression. He noticed how I pulled away from others with babies. He saw and felt my tears. He suffered too.

Dear Jill and Kevin,

It has been five months since you were born, Jill. The time has been so long and lonely. The other day I had a group of women at my house for a sewing club meeting. One of the women brought along her seven-month-old daughter. It was so awful. I am sure she didn't mean to hurt me so, but it hurt just the same. There was another little girl there as well. She was seventeen months old, a toddler. Your big brother kept pushing her and taking toys away from her. I had never seen him act like that. I would correct him, but he would do it again. I got so angry at him!

Finally, I pulled him into the other room and asked him what was the matter with him. He told me he hated that little girl. Then he asked me if you, Jill, were still in heaven.

Now I understood. I told him yes, you were in heaven. He was feeling the same envy and hurt I was. He just could not put it into words at the age of four. Everybody hurts.

Love,
Mommy

The whole process of this grief did not merely shake my faith; it challenged it in every way. I got so angry and questioned God and God's plan. I never lost faith in the truth that God was in charge and loved me, but I certainly felt God had an awfully cruel way of showing it to me at that time. This grief also challenged my identity. Who was I now? What was I supposed to do with my life? How was I supposed to cope and live out the rest of my days?

Dear Kevin and Jill,

It is a new year. I guess that is supposed to mean there is hope or a chance for new possibilities. I do not have much faith in that. I feel so alone. No one can fill my needs...my needs of desire, challenge, purpose, relief from this loneliness. The list goes on.

Maybe this is what happens to a person's self esteem and confidence when their children die. Maybe it just happens to women, to mothers. Maybe it has just happened to me. All I know is my confidence is shaken. I am terrified to go back to school. Terrified to stay at home with all those long empty hours. I am petrified of reaching out to someone and yet I know what I am doing is not working. I wish I knew what the answers are. I feel so all alone in it all.

Love,
Mommy

Time does heal, but it also brings fading memories. That hurts too.

Dear Kevin and Jill,

My memory is so bad. I try to remember how it felt to hold you and all I feel is such an ache. I try to remember your beautiful hands and fingers, Jill. It does not seem real. I try to remember the sounds of your cries, but I cannot hear them anymore.

Now your daddy is talking about moving again. It has only been nine months since you died, Jill. When we moved here, nine months after you died, Kevin, people did not know our story or our pain. It was so hard. Then you were born, Jill, and they shared in your death and our grief.

Now he is asking me to move again where the story of both of you is unknown. Move to a place where you are just a memory I talk of, not a part of their reality. I am not sure I can do it. Not again.

Love,

Mommy

Chapter 8

The Road to Healing

I returned once again to the therapist that helped me work through some of my grief after Kevin died. She was available to me and it was easier to return to her than to retell my story all over again. It was almost a year after Jill's death before I went. Somehow, I had decided in my head that if I had done this grief thing once, I could do it again. Also, I had been so wrapped up in my husband's depression; I felt there was no time for me to take care of me. With the help of medication, he was doing better. I finally realized I had better take my turn.

I know a great many people who grieve without the assistance of professionals. They find others to lean on. I was stubborn and proud and refused to lean on others. I kept that stoic facade up for so long that I couldn't be weak in front of anyone. It took its toll on me. It was okay for me to be weak in front of my therapist. She affirmed my fears and doubts. She didn't throw away my anger, telling me it was wrong. She accepted me and helped me see that I was not crazy. She helped me see that it was okay to love myself and not take the blame for everything that was so wrong in my life. This realization was a beautiful gift she gave me.

On the first anniversary of Jill's death, we tried a different approach. Our little, incomplete family drove to Minneapolis and stayed in a motel room. It didn't turn out to be family time like I hoped. My husband slept. My son and I tried to swim in the pool, but he was scared of the water. We went back to the room only to be yelled at for being loud. We had two beds in that room. My husband insisted that he have one and my son and I share the other. If I was not sure of it before, I was then. Although we stayed together for a while longer, I knew my marriage was over.

I returned to college that spring. I took only one course in the graduate psychology program. It was a course entitled "Psychology of Dysfunctional Families." I tried one more time to understand this dysfunctional relationship I shared with my husband. I worked hard as I wanted so desperately to succeed and learn. The final requirement for that class was a research paper on family and dysfunction. I chose to write about the dysfunction that grief can bring to a family– specifically sibling grief. Intellectualizing my grief seemed to help me. I learned a great deal in the process of writing that paper.

Dear Kevin and Jill,

Mommy has been so busy with her paper. I just love this class. I am learning and feel a part of something again. I am only gone four hours on Tuesday and Thursday afternoons. I feel guilty for leaving your big brother for that long, but it has been so good for me.

Our professor introduced a psych theory called bioenergetics. This theory says that any psychological condition or trauma will always manifest itself in your physical self. It was like I was struck over the head with a bat!

Remember when I was pregnant with you, Kevin– I got these awful warts on my hands? I had never had warts before and I have not had them since.

And then when I was pregnant with you, Jill– I got this horrible rash on my hands. I could not even wear my wedding ring. My hands would not heal when I was pregnant and it was not until after you died that they finally healed. I talked to my professor after class, explaining what happened. She thought it might be a physical sign of me trying to reach out for something I so desperately wanted. I thought of it as trying to hold on to something I knew I could not have.

Quite a discovery.

I love you.

Love,

Mommy

My husband, son, and I moved again. This time to a small town in northeastern Minnesota called Askov. It was eighteen months after Jill died. Once again, I was faced with telling my story to others or burying it deep inside of me. Neither option appealed to me. I had returned to full time work. That allowed me to keep busy and distant from my grief. My job was very demanding, taking most of my energy. I changed jobs a few months after the move. I ran across one of those stress charts where they give numerical totals for every stressful event in a person's life. I had the death of two children, a job change, and a move. No wonder I was a walking ball of nerves. I was off the charts!

I knew with my job change that I had found a stable income. I waited out my year of probationary status at work and filed for divorce. We were virtually forced into marriage counseling by my husband's supervisor, the bishop. My husband had refused all my previous attempts I had made to have him attend counseling with me. But now that his boss had recommended it strongly, he was willing. It was a blessing as it helped to reassure me that I deserved to be happy and fulfilled. The statistics say that about fifty percent of couples that lose a child end up in divorce. The rate goes up drastically for couples that lose more than one child. We too became a statistic.

How I ached for someone with whom to share my sorrow.

Dear Kevin and Jill,
Tonight
Tonight I hurt
Tonight I want you to hold me and let the tears flow
Tonight I want you to help me weep with my whole heart so I can heal
Tonight I want you close to me, to hold me close to you
let me know I am loved
that my pain is real
Sometimes I fear that since my pain is always saved for my moments of isolation
it is not a reality
Please think of me tonight
Be with me tonight
if only in my dreams
Love,
Mommy

There is no easy answer for healing. For me it meant some therapy, time, prayers, physical exercise, and a change in my marriage. The condition of my troubled marriage only worsened with grief. I know that when I left that marriage, I finally had the opportunity to truly grieve. I was no longer responsible for caring for another adult with no care in return. I was responsible for myself and my seven-year-old child, who now faced yet another loss in his short life. I was acutely aware of all his losses.

I did find healing. It took some time. I like to joke by saying that God finally came around and realized how much I hurt. That is really not the way it is. In some way, I have come to terms with God's will. I cannot say I wished for it, but I have learned to accept it and now, some time later, can appreciate how my life has been enriched.

I used to pray for a miracle. It would fill me with anger when others shared how their child had been saved by the power of prayer and a miracle. I prayed as hard as I could. It took me a long time to realize I was given a miracle. The miracle is that my babies did not suffer in this imperfect world, but instead were able to go to their heavenly home where they would not feel pain or disappointment. I take comfort in that.

I am not afraid to tell others about my anger toward God. I believe He can bear my anger and understand the pain in my heart that drives it. What a blessing that has been for me.

I remarried two years after my divorce. My husband Scott and I are so very happy. I have found the person whom I was searching for in the poem *Tonight.* We are partners in life, good and bad. Shortly after we were married, we learned we were expecting a child. We had not planned this. I do not think I could have planned a pregnancy. The medical experts had advised me not to try again. I had agreed. Despite this, we were blessed to have a healthy daughter. She is a joy; hence, we named her Joyce.

I learned I was pregnant again nine months later. I had only known about the baby for one week when I felt a cramping pain in my abdomen. I was painting the kitchen walls. I put down the roller and climbed down off the ladder. I knew in my heart what had happened. I had lost the baby due to a miscarriage. This too was a learning and grieving process. It was different from my other children's deaths. I was able to share my grief with my husband. We worked through those days together. My faith in God had also become stronger and I knew, somehow, I would feel hope again.

A few months later, we learned we were expecting another baby. A beautiful boy was born. His name is Jacob.

I now have a family of six children. Three are on this earth and three are in heaven. I remember reading books written by people who had lost babies and went on to have healthy children. I was so certain that the reason they could move on or heal was that they had an opportunity to have joy again. I will not lie. Joy is easier to grasp now that I have two more healthy children and a loving husband.

My grief is a dull ache now. I follow the example of that elderly woman who I heard about when Kevin died, to set aside the birthdays of my lost children and be good to myself. I expect very little of myself on those days. I have learned to love all the parts of me– even the parts that sometimes hold a bit of anger or self-pity. I have made amends with God. God loved me through out my struggle. I needed to return to faith. It wasn't difficult to find God, God was waiting for me.

He will wait for you too.

Julie S. Domogalla

A Happy Ending?

The woods speak to me
of quiet beauty, of majestic courage, of singleness of purpose.
My dreams are to carry my story to others
to share my discovery and pain
yet I am so terrified to do so
my life journey is not yet complete
Where is the happy ending?
There is no happy ending, no sunset or magical cure
only a sure dose of reality
Where I go from here is unknown
but I will continue on
knowing that life is never static unless we allow it to be
that my life will continue to unfold new joys if I open myself to them
that my pain and grief of yesterday has fed me with a deeper, clearer
appreciation for today
still, calm and dense like the majestic forest that surrounds me
what better joy could there be?

Epilogue

Grief Never Ends

Grief is hard work. It never ends. Somehow, I found a place in my heart for it to stay. Most days, it is a part of me, but not the dominant part of me. But there are reminders and situations that make it all resurface again.

It was five years ago. It had been ten and twelve years since my children's deaths. I received a phone call from my friend in Wisconsin. My children were buried next to his wife. There had been some confusion and miscalculations about space in the burial plot and it seemed that Kevin and Jill's remains would need to be excavated and interred somewhere else.

It was an excruciating process of death certificates, funeral homes, and waivers, but finally my husband and I drove to Wisconsin to get my children's tiny caskets. We had all agreed– my husband and I, and my ex-husband– that the children should now be buried closer to where we live, and a cemetery in our area was decided upon.

I wrote the following essay about this experience. It was printed in the local paper. Many people; people who never knew Kevin and Jill responded in sympathy and love. Once again, writing was part of my healing process.

Moving Day

Today was moving day. I hate moving. I moved so many times during my college and young adult years. I swore I would not continue to move like that in my life. I have lived in my present home longer than any place with the exception of where I grew up. It is nice to be home!

This moving day was different, however. We moved two of my children home, to Askov. I had two infant children, Kevin and Jill, who died. They were born alive and died from complications due to abnormal lung tissue. Kevin was five weeks old when he died; Jill lived two days. They died in much the same way at the same hospital with the same attending specialist. I pulled the ventilator tube from each of their mouths when they died. That was the one thing I could do for them– release them from their medically induced existence. I held them in my arms and said good-bye. That was ten and twelve years ago.

Two weeks ago I got a call from an old friend. My children were buried next to his wife, also a dear friend. We often had talked of how Margaret would love to care for them. He had a difficult time telling me that my babies needed to be exhumed and moved from their place of burial in Wisconsin. The details aren't important. People are human. Mistakes and misjudgments are made.

When the news was broken to me, I knew almost immediately that it was time for them to be closer to our home. To say this was an easy decision would be inaccurate. This process of documents, certificates and burial arrangements was not something I cared to do again. I met two members of the cemetery board at the local cemetery in our small town to find an appropriate spot. This was no easy task for two older gentlemen and one woman reliving some very painful days. If you will pardon the reference; the whole situation unearthed a lot of feelings that had been quieted for some time now.

When the decision was made to bury Kevin in Wisconsin, it seemed a logical choice. That was the place he had lived his short life and we had felt so much love and acceptance from people there. Kevin was different in many ways, but not just the obvious ones. He was born without arms or legs...some people came to stare at him. Luckily, most came to love him. I remember going shopping for something to wear to his baptism. He was wrapped in a blanket in the stroller and the clerk noted what a *perfect* baby he was. She had no idea how her words touched me. Kevin had abilities beyond his short life. He turned his head to his name at two weeks old. He smiled and seemed to tell me things through his eyes during those long nights we shared as he struggled in this life. He touched the lives of so many people across the country as friends and relatives told me continually. Somehow he was a source of hope for others in his short five weeks of life.

Then almost two years later, Jill was born. She too had limb abnormalities in her legs. But she had the longest fingers on the most beautiful hands I have ever seen on a baby. She was six weeks premature. She lived only forty-seven hours on this earth, but she looked at me, her mother, and I heard her cry. I know my daughter's voice and she saw her Mommy if only for a fleeting moment before she was sedated and intubated. Some people never get even these brief moments of joy with their child. I am so very grateful for those memories. Naturally, upon her death, the idea came to place her along side her brother and hence they were both buried next to my dear friend Margaret.

So today– after a great deal of planning and phone calls, tears, and memories– my husband, Scott, and I went to get them and bring them home. We transported the two small caskets, carefully wrapped in dark plastic, along with the headstones, to Askov. It is strange how they say that time heals all wounds. I had forgotten how small their caskets were. Somehow they seemed bigger on the days of their funerals. I questioned what kind of mother I was that I could not recall every detail of their burial and funeral.

Time fades memories as it helps to heal. Yet I know that is unrealistic...maybe unhealthy too; to dwell on every detail. Life continues on, whether we are ready or not.

We placed their tiny caskets in the plot and set the stones. People driving by later asked me what we were doing in the cemetery on that day. "Moving my children," I answered. People I did not know well reached out in compassion. Others sent cards or offered their support even though they never knew my little ones. Grace is everywhere if we open our hearts and eyes to see it.

So Kevin and Jill are now buried in the Bethlehem Lutheran Cemetery in Askov. I know that every April and July (their birthdays) I can go to the cemetery if I choose. This was very difficult before because of the distance involved. They never lived in Askov. Yet it is, in a way, their home– because it is my home. I know they are in a different home now. I hope to join them there someday.

It was such a long painful day. There are a lot of resurfaced memories...some good, most of them painful and sad.

Today was moving day. I hate moving. It is nice to be home. My whole family is home now.

Photos

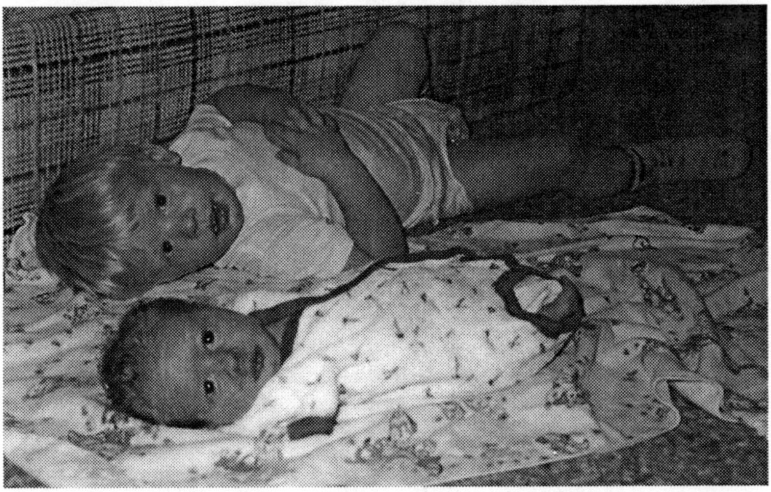

Kevin 3 weeks old with his big brother Jim age 23 months

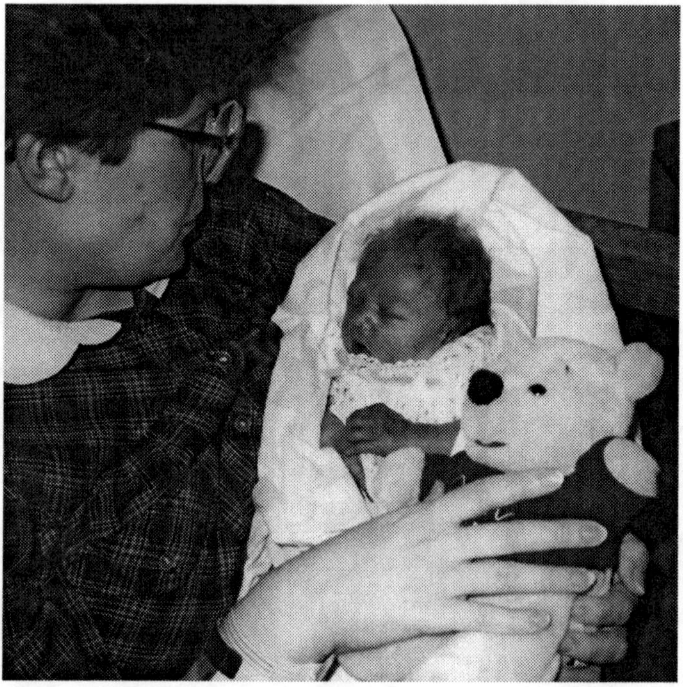

My last few minutes with my daughter Jill

Jim, Joyce and Jacob

Printed in the United States
109275LV00010B/18/A